Building a Successful Ebay Dropshipping for Beginners

How to Sell on Ebay without Holding An Inventory:
An E-Commerce 101 Guide To Grow Your Own Home
Based Reselling Business

Nancy D. Avant

Table Of Contents

Introduction

Welcome to the world of eBay dropshipping in 2024 and beyond! If you're an aspiring entrepreneur seeking a low-risk, high-profit venture in the realm of eCommerce, you're in the right place. In this guide, we'll embark on a journey through the ins and outs of dropshipping on eBay, tailored specifically for beginners like yourself.

Understanding eBay Dropshipping

First things first, let's demystify the concept of eBay dropshipping. Simply put, it's an innovative retail fulfillment method where sellers, like you, don't need to maintain inventory. Instead, you list products for sale on eBay and, upon receiving orders, forward them to third-party suppliers who handle shipping directly to your customers. This model offers unparalleled flexibility and scalability, making it an ideal starting point for budding entrepreneurs.

Getting Started with eBay Dropshipping

Now, let's dive into the nitty-gritty of starting your eBay dropshipping journey. From creating your seller account to researching profitable products and finding reliable suppliers, we'll walk you through each step with clarity and precision. Understanding eBay's dropshipping policies is crucial to avoid any pitfalls, and we'll ensure you navigate them seamlessly.

Costs of Dropshipping on eBay

No business venture is without its financial considerations, and eBay dropshipping is no exception. We'll explore the various costs involved, including free listings, subscription fees, insertion fees, final value fees, and promotional fees. Armed with this knowledge, you'll be equipped to budget effectively and maximize your profitability.

Setting Up Your eBay Dropshipping Business

With the groundwork laid, it's time to set up your eBay dropshipping business for success. We'll delve into the intricacies of optimizing your product listings, managing inventory and orders efficiently, and providing stellar customer service. By the end of this section, you'll be ready to hit the ground running and start generating sales.

Strategies for Success

In the competitive landscape of eBay dropshipping, strategic thinking is key. We'll share proven strategies for marketing and promoting your products, building trust and reputation as a seller, and implementing pricing strategies that drive profitability. Whether you're a newcomer or a seasoned entrepreneur, these insights will set you on the path to success.

Navigating eBay Policies and Regulations

eBay has specific policies and regulations governing dropshipping, and compliance is essential for sustained success. We'll provide a comprehensive overview of eBay's policies, common pitfalls to avoid, and tips for maintaining compliance to safeguard your seller account.

Adapting to Changes in 2024

As we navigate the dynamic landscape of eCommerce in 2024, it's essential to stay abreast of changes and innovations. We'll discuss recent updates in eBay policies and features, strategies for adapting to market trends and competition and leveraging new tools and technologies to stay ahead of the curve.

Case Studies and Success Stories

What better way to glean insights than from real-life examples of successful eBay dropshipping businesses? We'll share inspiring case studies and success stories, highlighting lessons learned and best practices from experienced sellers. These anecdotes will serve as valuable inspiration as you embark on your own eBay dropshipping journey.

eBay dropshipping in 2024 offers a world of opportunities for aspiring entrepreneurs. Armed with the knowledge and insights shared in this guide, you're well-equipped to embark on your eBay dropshipping journey with confidence. Whether you're looking to supplement your income or build a thriving eCommerce empire, the sky's the limit in the world of eBay dropshipping.

So, without further ado, let's dive in and unlock the potential of eBay dropshipping in 2024!

Understanding eBay Dropshipping

In the world of eCommerce, dropshipping has emerged as a popular retail fulfillment method, offering entrepreneurs a low-risk, high-reward business model. Among the myriad platforms available for dropshipping, eBay stands out as a prominent player, attracting sellers and buyers alike with its vast marketplace and robust infrastructure. In this section, we'll delve deeper into what eBay dropshipping entails, why it's a compelling choice for aspiring entrepreneurs, and the benefits and challenges associated with this business model.

What is eBay Dropshipping?

eBay dropshipping is a retail fulfillment method where sellers list products for sale on the eBay marketplace without actually stocking inventory. Rather, upon receiving an order from a consumer, the seller buys the item directly from a third-party supplier and sends it to the buyer. Without ever touching the goods, the seller essentially serves as a middleman, facilitating the transaction between the supplier and the client.

This model offers several advantages, including low startup costs, minimal inventory management, and the ability to operate from anywhere with an internet connection. Sellers can leverage eBay's vast customer base and established reputation to reach a global audience, making it an attractive option for entrepreneurs looking to enter the world of eCommerce.

Why Choose eBay for Dropshipping?

eBay's prominence in the eCommerce landscape makes it an enticing platform for dropshipping. With millions of active buyers and a diverse range of products spanning various categories, eBay offers sellers unparalleled access to a vast marketplace. The platform's user-friendly interface, robust seller tools, and built-in traffic generation capabilities make it easy for sellers to list products, manage orders, and drive sales.

Moreover, eBay's global reach enables sellers to tap into international markets, expanding their customer base and revenue potential. With eBay's seller protection policies in place, sellers can rest assured that their transactions are secure, mitigating the risk of fraudulent activities and disputes.

Benefits of eBay Dropshipping

1. Low Startup Costs: Unlike traditional retail models that require substantial upfront investments in inventory, eBay dropshipping allows entrepreneurs to start with minimal capital. Since sellers only purchase products from suppliers after receiving orders from customers, there's no need to invest in stocking inventory upfront.

2. Minimal Inventory Management: Inventory management can be a time-consuming and resource-intensive aspect of running a retail business. With eBay dropshipping, sellers eliminate the need for storing, packaging, and shipping products, freeing up valuable time and resources to focus on other aspects of their business.

3. Scalability and Flexibility: eBay dropshipping provides merchants with unmatched scalability, enabling them to run their businesses from any location with an internet connection. Whether you're a stay-at-home parent, a digital nomad, or a budding entrepreneur, eBay dropshipping accommodates various lifestyles and schedules. Additionally, the scalability of the dropshipping model enables sellers to expand their product offerings and reach new markets without the constraints of physical inventory.

4. Access to a Global Marketplace: With millions of active buyers worldwide, eBay provides sellers with access to a vast and diverse customer base. Whether you're selling niche products or popular consumer goods, eBay's global reach allows you to connect with buyers from around the world, maximizing your sales potential.

5. Built-in Traffic and Marketing Tools: eBay's platform features built-in traffic generation and marketing tools, making it easier for sellers to attract customers and drive sales. From sponsored listings and promoted listings to eBay's robust search algorithm, sellers can leverage these tools to increase visibility and reach their target audience.

Challenges of eBay Dropshipping

1. Competition: With millions of sellers vying for attention on eBay's platform, competition can be fierce, especially in popular product categories. Standing out from the crowd and attracting customers requires strategic marketing and differentiation strategies.

2. Margin Compression: In a competitive marketplace like eBay, price wars and discounting can lead to margin compression, affecting sellers' profitability. Balancing competitive pricing with maintaining healthy profit margins is a constant challenge for eBay dropshippers.

3. Inventory Management and Supplier Reliability: While eBay dropshipping eliminates the need for stocking inventory, sellers must rely on third-party suppliers to fulfill orders promptly and accurately. Managing relationships with suppliers and ensuring reliable order fulfillment can be challenging, particularly when dealing with multiple suppliers.

4. eBay Policies and Regulations: eBay has specific policies and regulations governing dropshipping activities on its platform. Sellers must familiarize themselves with these policies and comply with eBay's guidelines to avoid account suspensions or penalties.

5. Customer Service and Returns: As the intermediary between customers and suppliers, eBay drop shippers are responsible for providing excellent customer service and handling returns and inquiries promptly. Managing customer expectations and resolving disputes effectively is crucial for maintaining a positive seller reputation.

Getting Started with eBay Dropshipping

Dropshipping on eBay is a lucrative business model that allows entrepreneurs to sell products without the need for inventory management or shipping logistics. It offers a low barrier to entry, making it an attractive option for beginners looking to start an online business. In this section, we'll explore the essential steps to kickstart your eBay dropshipping journey.

Creating a Seller Account on eBay

The first step to getting started with eBay dropshipping is creating a seller account. It's a straightforward process that involves providing basic information about yourself or your business, such as your name, address, and contact details. You'll also need to verify your identity and link a payment method to your account.

Once your seller account is set up, you can start listing products for sale on eBay. It's essential to familiarize yourself with eBay's seller policies and guidelines to ensure compliance and avoid any potential issues down the line. Additionally, consider investing in an eBay Store subscription for access to advanced selling tools and customization options.

Researching Profitable Products

One of the keys to success in eBay dropshipping is selecting the right products to sell. Conducting thorough market research is crucial to identify profitable niches and products with high demand and low competition. Start by exploring eBay's product categories and analyzing top-selling items to gain insights into consumer preferences and trends.

Utilize eBay's advanced search filters and tools like Terapeak to analyze sales data, track pricing trends, and identify popular keywords. Pay attention to product reviews, feedback, and seller ratings to gauge customer satisfaction and assess market demand accurately.

Consider factors like product availability, shipping costs, and potential profit margins when evaluating product options. Look for products with a reasonable selling price that allows for a competitive markup while remaining attractive to buyers.

Finding Reliable Suppliers

Once you've identified profitable products to sell, the next step is to find reliable suppliers or dropshipping partners. Building a network of trusted suppliers is essential for ensuring product quality, timely order fulfillment, and customer satisfaction.

Start by researching reputable dropshipping suppliers through online directories, wholesale marketplaces, or direct contact with manufacturers. Look for suppliers with a proven track record of reliability, quality control, and efficient shipping practices.

When evaluating potential suppliers, consider factors like product variety, pricing, minimum order quantities, shipping times, and return policies. Establish clear communication channels and negotiate pricing terms to ensure a mutually beneficial partnership.

It's also crucial to conduct due diligence and verify the legitimacy of potential suppliers to avoid scams or fraudulent activities. Request product samples, review supplier contracts, and seek feedback from other sellers or industry forums to vet suppliers effectively.

Understanding eBay's Dropshipping Policies

Before diving into eBay dropshipping, it's essential to familiarize yourself with eBay's dropshipping policies and guidelines. eBay has specific rules and regulations governing dropshipping practices to ensure a positive buying experience for customers and maintain the integrity of the marketplace.

Key aspects of eBay's dropshipping policies include:

- ***Product Availability***: Sellers are responsible for ensuring that listed items are in stock and available for immediate shipment. Avoid listing products that are out of stock or have extended shipping times to prevent order cancellations and negative feedback.

- *Delivery Times:* Sellers must provide accurate estimated delivery times to customers based on the chosen shipping method and supplier's processing times. Failure to meet delivery deadlines can result in buyer dissatisfaction and potential penalties from eBay.

- *Product Descriptions and Images*: Sellers are required to provide accurate and detailed product descriptions, including relevant information such as specifications, dimensions, and features. Use high-quality images to showcase products accurately and attractively.

- *Customer Service:* Sellers are responsible for handling customer inquiries, resolving issues, and providing timely support throughout the buying process. Maintain open communication with buyers, address any concerns promptly, and strive to deliver exceptional customer service.

- *Return Policies:* eBay's standard return policy applies to dropshipped items, allowing buyers to return items for a refund within a specified timeframe. Ensure clear and transparent return policies to facilitate smooth returns and refunds for customers.

By understanding and adhering to eBay's dropshipping policies, you can build a successful and compliant dropshipping business on the platform. Stay informed about policy updates and changes to ensure ongoing compliance and mitigate any potential risks or issues.

Costs of Dropshipping on eBay

Dropshipping on eBay offers a lucrative business opportunity with minimal upfront costs, making it an attractive option for entrepreneurs looking to start an online business. However, it's essential to understand the various costs associated with dropshipping on eBay to effectively budget and manage expenses. In this section, we'll explore the different costs involved in eBay dropshipping and provide insights into budgeting strategies for success.

Free Listings and Subscription Fees

eBay offers sellers the opportunity to list a certain number of items for free each month, depending on their seller status and subscription level. For example, eBay's Basic plan includes a set number of free listings per month, while higher-tier subscription plans like eBay Premium and eBay Anchor offer unlimited free listings.

Optimizing your listings and taking advantage of free listing opportunities can help reduce your upfront costs and maximize your selling potential on eBay. Focus on creating compelling product descriptions, utilizing high-quality images, and leveraging relevant keywords to attract potential buyers and drive sales.

Insertion Fees

In addition to free listings, eBay charges insertion fees for listing items beyond the allocated free listings included in your subscription plan. Insertion fees vary based on factors such as the item's category, listing format (auction-style or fixed price), and duration (listing duration).

To minimize insertion fees, consider strategically selecting the most relevant categories and listing formats for your products. Opt for fixed-price listings over auction-style listings for greater control over pricing and inventory management. Additionally, choose shorter listing durations to test product performance and adjust pricing or listings as needed without incurring additional fees.

Final Value Fees

eBay charges final value fees on the total selling price of an item, including shipping costs, once the item is sold. Final value fees typically range from 10% to 12% of the total transaction value, depending on the item category and subscription level.

When pricing your products, factor in final value fees to ensure a competitive yet profitable selling price. Consider incorporating shipping costs into your item prices to avoid higher final value fees on shipping charges. Additionally, explore eBay's fee structure and subscription plans to identify opportunities for cost savings and optimize your profit margins.

Promotional Fees

eBay offers various promotional tools and advertising options to help sellers increase visibility and drive sales for their listings. Promotional fees may include sponsored listings, promoted listings, and other advertising initiatives aimed at increasing listing visibility and attracting potential buyers.

While promotional fees can enhance listing visibility and increase sales potential, it's essential to evaluate the return on investment (ROI) of each promotional strategy. Monitor performance metrics like click-through rates (CTR), conversion rates, and sales attribution to assess the effectiveness of promotional activities and adjust your marketing strategy accordingly.

Other Considerations for Budgeting

In addition to the direct costs associated with eBay dropshipping, consider other factors that may impact your budget and overall profitability:

Shipping Costs: Factor in shipping costs, including packaging materials, postage fees, and carrier charges, when calculating your total expenses and profit margins. Explore shipping options and negotiate discounted rates with shipping carriers to minimize shipping costs and maximize profitability.

Currency Conversion and Transaction Fees: If selling internationally or dealing with buyers in different currencies, be mindful of currency conversion fees and transaction fees imposed by payment processors or financial institutions. Consider utilizing multi-currency payment solutions or currency conversion tools to mitigate currency-related costs and streamline international transactions.

Customer Service and Returns: Allocate resources for customer service support and returns management to handle inquiries, resolve issues, and facilitate returns and refunds effectively. Investing in excellent customer service can help build trust and loyalty among buyers, leading to positive feedback and repeat business.

Inventory Management: Implement efficient inventory management practices to minimize holding costs, prevent stock outs or overstock situations, and optimize inventory turnover. Utilize inventory management software or platforms to track inventory levels, monitor sales trends, and make data-driven decisions to manage your inventory effectively.

By understanding and budgeting for the various costs associated with dropshipping on eBay, you can develop a comprehensive financial plan and pricing strategy to maximize profitability and long-term success.

Monitor your expenses, track key performance indicators (KPIs), and continuously evaluate and adjust your business strategies to adapt to market dynamics and achieve your business goals.

Setting Up Your eBay Dropshipping Business

Setting up an eBay dropshipping business requires attention to detail and a well-thought-out strategy to ensure smooth operations and customer satisfaction. In this section, we'll delve into the crucial aspects of optimizing product listings, managing inventory and orders, fulfilling orders with suppliers, and providing excellent customer service.

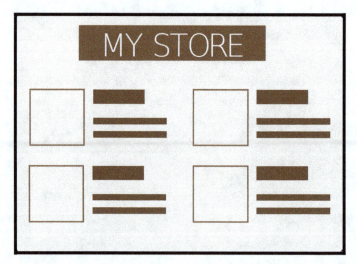

Optimizing Product Listings

Optimizing your product listings is essential for attracting potential buyers and maximizing sales on eBay. Here are some key strategies to optimize your listings effectively:

1. *Keyword Research:* Conduct thorough keyword research to identify relevant keywords and phrases that potential buyers are likely to search for. Incorporate these keywords naturally into your product titles and descriptions to improve visibility in search results.

2. *High-Quality Images:* Use high-quality images that accurately represent the product you're selling. Clear, well-lit photos from multiple angles can significantly enhance the appeal of your listings and instill confidence in potential buyers.

3. *Detailed Descriptions:* Provide detailed and accurate descriptions of your products, including key features, specifications, dimensions, and any other relevant information. Clear and informative descriptions help buyers make informed purchasing decisions and reduce the likelihood of returns or disputes.

4. *Competitive Pricing:* Research competitor pricing and set competitive prices for your products. Consider factors such as product quality, shipping costs, and seller reputation when determining your pricing strategy.

5. *Clear Shipping and Return Policies:* Clearly outline your shipping and return policies in your listings to set clear expectations for buyers. Provide information about shipping times, methods, and costs, as well as your return policy, to minimize confusion and potential disputes.

6. *Optimized Titles and Subtitles:* Craft compelling and descriptive product titles and subtitles that capture the attention of buyers and accurately convey the key selling points of your products. Use relevant keywords and phrases to improve search visibility and attract potential buyers.

7. *Utilize eBay Features:* Take advantage of eBay's listing features, such as item specifics, product identifiers, and variations, to provide detailed information about your products and enhance their visibility in search results.

By implementing these optimization strategies, you can create compelling product listings that attract buyers and drive sales on eBay.

Managing Inventory and Orders

Efficient inventory management is crucial for ensuring that you have an adequate supply of products to meet customer demand while minimizing the risk of overselling or stockouts.

Here's how to effectively manage your inventory and orders:

1. Track Inventory Levels: Implement a reliable inventory tracking system to monitor your stock levels in real time. Regularly update your inventory counts to accurately reflect the availability of products and avoid overselling.

2. Set Reorder Points: Establish reorder points for your products based on historical sales data and lead times from suppliers. Reorder products proactively to maintain optimal inventory levels and prevent stockouts.

3. Automate Order Processing: Utilize order management software or eBay's seller tools to automate order processing tasks, such as order confirmation, invoicing, and shipping label generation. Automation can streamline your operations and reduce manual errors.

4. Monitor Sales Trends: Analyze sales trends and patterns to identify top-selling products, seasonal fluctuations, and emerging trends. Adjust your inventory levels and product offerings accordingly to capitalize on opportunities and minimize excess inventory.

5. Coordinate with Suppliers: Maintain open communication with your suppliers to ensure timely replenishment of stock and address any issues or delays promptly. Establish clear expectations regarding lead times, order quantities, and shipping methods to streamline the ordering process.

6. Implement SKU System: Assign unique stock-keeping unit (SKU) numbers to each product to facilitate easy identification and organization of inventory. A standardized SKU system can streamline inventory management and order fulfillment processes.

By implementing effective inventory management practices, you can maintain optimal stock levels, minimize stockouts, and ensure timely order fulfillment for your eBay dropshipping business.

Fulfilling Orders with Suppliers

Fulfilling orders with suppliers is a critical aspect of the dropshipping process that requires efficient coordination and communication. Here's how to effectively fulfill orders with your suppliers:

1. Automate Order Forwarding: Set up automated processes to forward customer orders to your suppliers seamlessly. Utilize order management software or integrations to automate the order-forwarding process and minimize manual intervention.

2. Confirm Order Receipt: Confirm receipt of customer orders with your suppliers promptly to initiate order processing and fulfillment. Provide accurate order details, including product SKUs, quantities, and shipping addresses, to ensure smooth order processing.

3. *Monitor Order Status:* Monitor the status of orders with your suppliers closely to track order processing, shipping, and delivery. Maintain open communication with your suppliers to address any delays or issues that may arise during the fulfillment process.

4. *Provide Tracking Information:* Once orders are fulfilled and shipped by your suppliers, provide tracking information to your customers promptly. Communicate shipping updates and delivery timelines to keep customers informed and enhance their buying experience.

5. *Address Order Errors:* In the event of order errors or discrepancies, such as incorrect items shipped or shipping delays, work closely with your suppliers to resolve the issue promptly. Prioritize customer satisfaction by offering timely resolutions and updates to affected customers.

6. Evaluate Supplier Performance: Regularly evaluate the performance of your suppliers based on criteria such as order accuracy, shipping times, and communication responsiveness. Identify areas for improvement and address any issues or concerns with your suppliers proactively.

By establishing efficient processes for order fulfillment and maintaining strong relationships with your suppliers, you can ensure timely and accurate delivery of orders to your customers.

Dealing with Customer Service

Providing excellent customer service is paramount for building trust and credibility with buyers and fostering long-term customer relationships. Here's how to effectively handle customer service inquiries and issues:

1. *Prompt Communication:* Respond to customer inquiries and messages promptly to demonstrate responsiveness and professionalism. Aim to address customer inquiries within 24-48 hours to provide timely assistance and support.

2. *Resolve Issues Proactively:* Proactively identify and address any issues or concerns raised by customers, such as product inquiries, order status updates, or shipping delays. Offer personalized solutions and assistance to resolve customer issues promptly and effectively.

3. *Handle Returns and Refunds:* Establish clear return and refund policies and communicate them to customers upfront. Handle returns and refunds promptly and courteously, following eBay's guidelines and policies to ensure a positive customer experience.

4. Manage Feedback and Reviews: Monitor customer feedback and reviews regularly and respond to feedback promptly, whether positive or negative. Address any negative feedback or concerns raised by customers professionally and strive to resolve issues amicably.

5. Provide Exceptional Service: Go above and beyond to provide exceptional service and exceed customer expectations. Offer personalized recommendations, assistance with product selection, and proactive communication throughout the purchasing process to enhance the customer experience.

6. Learn from Customer Feedback: Gather insights from customer feedback and reviews to identify areas for improvement and enhance your products and services continually. Use feedback to refine your offerings, address customer pain points, and deliver a better overall experience.

By prioritizing customer service and implementing effective strategies for communication, issue resolution, and feedback management, you can build a positive reputation as a reliable and trustworthy eBay seller.

Strategies for Success in eBay Dropshipping

Dropshipping on eBay presents a unique opportunity for entrepreneurs to build a successful online business without the need for significant upfront investment in inventory. However, achieving success in this competitive marketplace requires strategic planning, effective marketing, and a focus on customer satisfaction. In this section, we'll explore key strategies for success in eBay dropshipping, covering marketing tactics, reputation building, pricing strategies, and operational efficiency tips.

Marketing and Promoting Your Products

Effective marketing is essential for driving traffic to your eBay listings, increasing visibility, and ultimately boosting sales. Here are some marketing strategies to consider for promoting your dropshipping products on eBay:

1. Optimized Product Listings: Craft compelling product titles and descriptions that highlight key features, benefits, and unique selling points. Utilize high-quality images and videos to showcase your products from multiple angles and provide detailed product information to help potential buyers make informed purchasing decisions.

2. *Keyword Optimization:* Conduct keyword research to identify relevant keywords and phrases that potential buyers are likely to use when searching for products on eBay. Incorporate these keywords strategically into your product titles, descriptions, and item specifics to improve search visibility and attract targeted traffic to your listings.

3. *Promoted Listings:* Leverage eBay's promoted listings feature to increase the visibility of your listings in search results and attract more potential buyers. Set an advertising budget and select the listings you want to promote based on performance metrics and profitability.

4. *Social Media Marketing:* Utilize social media platforms like Facebook, Instagram, and Pinterest to promote your eBay listings and engage with your target audience. Share visually appealing content, run targeted advertising campaigns, and interact with followers to drive traffic to your eBay store and increase sales.

5. Email Marketing: Build an email list of interested buyers and subscribers and leverage email marketing campaigns to promote new product launches, special promotions, and exclusive offers. Personalize your email content, segment your audience, and use compelling call-to-action (CTA) to encourage recipients to visit your eBay store and make a purchase.

Building Trust and Reputation as a Seller

Establishing trust and credibility as a seller is crucial for attracting buyers, gaining their confidence, and building a loyal customer base. Here are some strategies for building trust and reputation as a seller on eBay:

1. Provide Excellent Customer Service: Respond promptly to customer inquiries, address concerns or issues promptly, and provide clear and transparent communication throughout the buying process. Offer hassle-free returns and refunds to instill confidence in your buyers and demonstrate your commitment to customer satisfaction.

2. *Maintain High Standards of Product Quality:* Partner with reliable suppliers and vendors who offer high-quality products and ensure timely order fulfillment and delivery. Conduct quality control checks on products before shipping them to customers to minimize the risk of returns or negative feedback.

3. *Earn Positive Feedback and Ratings:* Encourage satisfied customers to leave positive feedback and ratings on your eBay listings by providing exceptional service, delivering products as described, and exceeding customer expectations. Monitor feedback and ratings regularly and address any negative feedback or disputes promptly to mitigate potential reputational damage.

4. Build a Professional Brand Image: Create a professional eBay store with a cohesive brand identity, including a customized store design, logo, and branding elements that reflect your brand's values and personality. Consistency in branding helps reinforce your brand identity and credibility as a seller.

5. Engage with the eBay Community: Participate actively in the eBay community by joining seller forums, participating in discussions, and sharing insights and experiences with fellow sellers. Networking with other sellers, sharing best practices, and seeking advice from experienced sellers can help you learn and grow as a seller on eBay.

Pricing Strategies for Profitability

Pricing your products competitively yet profitably is essential for maximizing sales and profitability in eBay dropshipping. Here are some pricing strategies to consider:

1. *Competitive Pricing Analysis:* Research competitors' prices and analyze market trends to determine the optimal pricing strategy for your products. Set a competitive price for your goods to draw in customers while maintaining a respectable profit margin.

2. *Dynamic Pricing:* Implement dynamic pricing strategies based on factors such as demand, competition, and seasonality to adjust prices in real time and maximize sales opportunities. Utilize pricing automation tools or software to monitor market conditions and adjust prices automatically to stay competitive.

3. *Bundle Pricing:* Create product bundles or value packs by bundling complementary products together and offering them at a discounted price compared to purchasing items individually. Bundle pricing can increase the perceived value of your offerings and incentivize buyers to make larger purchases.

4. *Tiered Pricing:* Offer tiered pricing discounts based on order quantity or purchase volume to encourage bulk purchases and increase average order value. Implement tiered pricing structures with graduated discounts for higher order quantities to incentivize customers to buy more and save.

5. *Promotional Pricing:* Run limited-time promotions, flash sales, or seasonal discounts to create a sense of urgency and drive sales. Offer exclusive discounts or coupon codes to loyal customers or subscribers to reward their loyalty and encourage repeat purchases.

Tips for Efficient Operations and Growth

Efficient operations are essential for managing your eBay dropshipping business effectively and driving sustainable growth. Here are some tips for optimizing your operations and maximizing efficiency:

1. Streamlined Order Processing: Implement streamlined order processing workflows and utilize order management software or tools to automate order processing, tracking, and fulfillment. Optimize order processing times to ensure timely order fulfillment and enhance customer satisfaction.

2. Effective Inventory Management: Adopt efficient inventory management practices to track inventory levels, monitor stock availability, and prevent stockouts or overstock situations. Utilize inventory management software to track inventory movement, forecast demand, and optimize inventory levels to minimize holding costs.

3. *Continuous Market Research:* Stay informed about market trends, consumer preferences, and competitor activities through continuous market research and analysis. Monitor eBay's marketplace trends, analyze sales data, and adapt your product offerings and pricing strategies accordingly to stay competitive.

4. *Invest in Technology and Tools:* Invest in technology, software, and tools that can streamline your operations, automate repetitive tasks, and improve efficiency. Utilize analytics tools, accounting software, and marketing automation platforms to gain insights, track performance, and optimize business operations.

5. *Focus on Customer Retention:* Prioritize customer retention strategies to build long-term relationships with your customers and encourage repeat purchases. Implement customer loyalty programs, offer personalized recommendations, and provide exceptional customer service to enhance customer satisfaction and loyalty.

By implementing these strategies and best practices, you can enhance your chances of success in eBay dropshipping, attract more customers, drive sales, and build a profitable and sustainable online business. Continuously evaluate and refine your strategies, adapt to market dynamics, and remain agile to capitalize on emerging opportunities and drive long-term growth and success.

Navigating eBay Policies and Regulations in Dropshipping

Dropshipping on eBay offers immense opportunities for entrepreneurs to start and grow their businesses without the need for extensive inventory or logistical overhead.

However, success in this endeavor is contingent upon a thorough understanding and adherence to eBay's policies and regulations governing dropshipping activities. In this section, we will delve into the intricacies of eBay's policies, common mistakes to avoid, and tips for maintaining compliance to ensure the smooth operation of your dropshipping business.

Understanding eBay's Policies on Dropshipping

Before embarking on your dropshipping journey on eBay, it is imperative to familiarize yourself with the platform's policies regarding dropshipping activities. eBay has specific guidelines and regulations in place to maintain a fair and transparent marketplace for buyers and sellers alike. Some key aspects of eBay's dropshipping policies include:

1. Seller Performance Standards: eBay holds sellers accountable for maintaining high levels of customer satisfaction and service. Sellers must adhere to performance metrics such as on-time shipping, tracking upload, low defect rate, and positive feedback to maintain a good standing on the platform.

2. *Product Sourcing and Fulfillment:* eBay requires sellers to fulfill orders directly from their inventory or through authorized suppliers. Dropshipping from third-party retailers or marketplaces is permitted, provided sellers ensure timely delivery, accurate item descriptions, and customer satisfaction.

3. *Shipping and Delivery Times:* Sellers are responsible for providing accurate shipping information and meeting eBay's delivery timeframes. Failure to adhere to shipping deadlines or prolonged delivery times can result in negative feedback, low seller ratings, and potential account suspension.

4. *Product Quality and Authenticity:* Sellers must accurately represent the quality, condition, and authenticity of the products they list on eBay. Misleading listings, counterfeit goods, or misrepresented items can result in buyer dissatisfaction, disputes, and account suspension.

5. Communication with Buyers: Effective communication with buyers is essential for building trust and resolving issues promptly. Sellers must respond to buyer inquiries, address concerns or complaints, and provide timely updates throughout the transaction process.

Avoiding Common Mistakes and Policy Violations

While dropshipping on eBay offers numerous benefits, there are common pitfalls and mistakes that sellers must avoid to prevent policy violations and account suspension. Some common mistakes include:

1. Misleading Product Descriptions: Sellers must accurately describe the products they list on eBay, including detailed descriptions, specifications, and images. Misleading or inaccurate product descriptions can lead to buyer dissatisfaction and disputes.

2. *Delayed Order Fulfillment:* Timely order fulfillment is crucial for maintaining customer satisfaction and meeting eBay's shipping deadlines. Sellers must ensure prompt order processing, shipment, and delivery to avoid negative feedback and low seller ratings.

3. *Non-Compliant Dropshipping Practices:* eBay prohibits certain dropshipping practices that may compromise the buyer experience or violate platform policies. Sellers must refrain from using third-party retailers or marketplaces as dropshipping suppliers without authorization, as this can lead to account suspension.

4. *Poor Customer Service:* Providing excellent customer service is essential for building trust and reputation as a seller on eBay. Sellers must respond to buyer inquiries promptly, address concerns or complaints effectively, and prioritize customer satisfaction to avoid negative feedback and disputes.

5. *Violation of eBay's Policies:* Sellers must familiarize themselves with eBay's policies and regulations governing dropshipping activities and ensure compliance at all times. Violating eBay's policies can result in account suspension, loss of selling privileges, and financial penalties.

Tips for Maintaining Compliance and Avoiding Suspension

To ensure the smooth operation of your dropshipping business on eBay and avoid potential policy violations or account suspension, consider the following tips:

1. *Read and Understand eBay's Policies:* Take the time to thoroughly read and understand eBay's policies and regulations governing dropshipping activities. Familiarize yourself with the dos and don'ts of dropshipping on eBay to ensure compliance with platform guidelines.

2. Select Reliable Suppliers: Partner with reputable and reliable suppliers who offer high-quality products, timely order fulfillment, and excellent customer service. Choose suppliers with a track record of reliability and integrity to mitigate the risk of shipping delays or product quality issues.

3. Provide Accurate Product Descriptions: Ensure that your product listings accurately represent the quality, condition, and specifications of the items you are selling. Use clear and detailed product descriptions, images, and item specifics to provide buyers with accurate information and set realistic expectations.

4. Maintain Transparent Communication: Communicate transparently with buyers throughout the transaction process, from order placement to delivery. Provide timely updates on order status, shipping tracking information, and any potential delays to keep buyers informed and minimize disputes.

5. *Monitor Performance Metrics:* Regularly monitor your seller performance metrics on eBay, including feedback ratings, defect rates, and shipping metrics. Address any performance issues promptly and take proactive measures to improve your seller performance and maintain compliance with eBay's standards.

Adapting to Changes in 2024

The landscape of eBay dropshipping is constantly evolving, with new policies, features, market trends, and technological advancements shaping the way sellers conduct their businesses. In 2024, staying competitive and successful in the realm of eBay dropshipping requires a proactive approach to adapting to changes and leveraging new opportunities.

We will explore the key strategies for adapting to changes in 2024, including updates in eBay policies and features, strategies for staying ahead of market trends and competition, and the integration of new tools and technologies for success.

Updates and Changes in eBay Policies and Features

eBay, like any other online marketplace, frequently updates its policies and features to enhance the buyer and seller experience, improve platform security, and address emerging issues in the e-commerce landscape.

As a dropshipping seller on eBay, it is essential to stay informed about these updates and adapt your business practices accordingly. Some common updates and changes in eBay policies and features that sellers may encounter in 2024 include:

1. Policy Updates: eBay may introduce changes to its dropshipping policies to address new challenges or improve the overall seller experience.

These updates may include revisions to seller performance standards, product sourcing guidelines, or shipping requirements. Sellers must stay updated on these policy changes and adjust their dropshipping practices to remain compliant with eBay's guidelines.

2. *Feature Enhancements:* eBay regularly introduces new features and tools to enhance the selling experience for sellers. These features may include improved listing tools, enhanced analytics and reporting capabilities, or streamlined order management systems. Sellers should leverage these new features to optimize their dropshipping operations, improve efficiency, and stay competitive in the marketplace.

3. *Platform Security Measures:* To protect the integrity of the marketplace and ensure a safe shopping environment for buyers, eBay may implement new security measures or fraud prevention mechanisms. Sellers should familiarize themselves with these security protocols and take proactive steps to safeguard their accounts and transactions from potential threats or fraudulent activities.

Strategies for Adapting to Market Trends and Competition

The e-commerce landscape is constantly evolving, with shifting consumer preferences, emerging market trends, and evolving competitive dynamics shaping the industry. To stay ahead in the world of eBay dropshipping in 2024, sellers must adopt strategic approaches to adapt to market trends and outpace the competition. Some key strategies for adapting to market trends and competition include:

1. Market Research and Analysis: Conducting thorough market research and analysis is crucial for identifying emerging trends, consumer preferences, and competitive insights. Sellers should monitor industry trends, analyze competitor strategies, and gather data on customer behavior to inform their dropshipping decisions and stay ahead of the curve.

2. Product Diversification: Diversifying your product offerings can help you capitalize on new market opportunities, cater to evolving consumer preferences, and mitigate risks associated with changes in demand or competition. Sellers should regularly assess their product portfolio, explore new product categories, and identify niche markets to expand their reach and maximize sales potential.

3. Dynamic Pricing Strategies: Pricing is a key determinant of competitiveness in the e-commerce landscape. Adopting dynamic pricing strategies, such as pricing optimization algorithms or real-time pricing adjustments, can help sellers remain competitive, maximize profitability, and respond effectively to changes in market demand and competition.

4. Customer Experience Enhancement:
Providing an exceptional customer experience is
essential for retaining customers, driving repeat
business, and differentiating your brand in a
competitive marketplace. Sellers should focus on
enhancing the overall shopping experience through
personalized customer service, seamless order
fulfillment, and hassle-free returns and refund
processes.

Leveraging New Tools and Technologies for Success

Advancements in technology continue to
revolutionize the e-commerce industry, offering
sellers new opportunities to streamline operations,
enhance efficiency, and drive growth.

In 2024, sellers can leverage a wide range of tools
and technologies to optimize their dropshipping
businesses and stay ahead of the competition. Some

key tools and technologies for success in eBay dropshipping include:

1. *Automation Software:* Automation software can streamline various aspects of the dropshipping process, including inventory management, order processing, and customer communication. Sellers can leverage automation tools to reduce manual workload, improve operational efficiency, and scale their businesses more effectively.

2. *Data Analytics Platforms:* Data analytics platforms enable sellers to gather valuable insights into customer behavior, sales trends, and market dynamics. By analyzing data metrics such as sales performance, customer demographics, and product demand, sellers can make informed decisions, optimize their strategies, and identify new growth opportunities.

3. *E-commerce Integration Solutions:* E-commerce integration solutions allow sellers to seamlessly integrate their eBay dropshipping operations with other sales channels, such as online marketplaces, e-commerce platforms, and fulfillment centers. By synchronizing inventory, orders, and shipping information across multiple channels, sellers can streamline operations, improve inventory management, and reach a broader audience of potential buyers.

4. Artificial Intelligence (AI) Tools: AI-powered tools and algorithms can help sellers optimize various aspects of their dropshipping businesses, including product recommendations, pricing strategies, and customer support. By leveraging AI technology, sellers can personalize the shopping experience, optimize pricing for maximum profitability, and automate customer service processes to enhance overall efficiency.

Adapting to changes in 2024 and staying ahead in the world of eBay dropshipping requires a proactive approach to navigating policy updates, embracing market trends, and leveraging new tools and technologies for success.

By staying informed about eBay's policies and features, adopting strategic approaches to market trends and competition, and integrating innovative tools and technologies into their businesses, sellers can position themselves for growth and profitability in the dynamic landscape of eBay dropshipping.

Case Studies and Success Stories

In the world of eBay dropshipping, success stories and case studies serve as valuable sources of inspiration and learning for aspiring entrepreneurs and experienced sellers alike. By examining real-life examples of successful eBay dropshipping businesses, analyzing their strategies, and understanding the lessons learned from experienced sellers, individuals can gain insights into the key factors that contribute to success in this competitive marketplace.

Real-Life Examples of Successful eBay Dropshipping Businesses

1. Case Study 1: The Power of Niche Selection

Case Study Summary: Sarah, a seasoned eBay dropshipper, identified a profitable niche in eco-friendly home products. By conducting thorough market research and identifying consumer demand for sustainable living solutions, Sarah curated a selection of high-quality, environmentally friendly products and optimized her eBay listings with compelling product descriptions and images.

Leveraging social media marketing and influencer partnerships, Sarah successfully attracted eco-conscious consumers to her eBay store, driving sales and establishing herself as a reputable seller in the niche.

Key Takeaways: This case study highlights the importance of niche selection in eBay dropshipping. By identifying a niche with high demand and low competition, sellers can carve out a unique market position, attract targeted customers, and drive sales growth.

2. Case Study 2: The Power of Automation

Case Study Summary: John, a full-time eBay dropshipper, leveraged automation tools to streamline his dropshipping operations and scale his business efficiently. By implementing automated inventory management software, order processing systems, and customer communication tools, John significantly reduced manual workload and operational costs while improving order accuracy and customer satisfaction.

With more time and resources freed up, John focused on expanding his product catalog, optimizing his listings, and exploring new sales channels, leading to exponential growth in his eBay dropshipping business.

Key Takeaways: This case study underscores the importance of automation in eBay dropshipping. By automating repetitive tasks and processes, sellers can enhance efficiency, reduce operational overhead, and allocate more time and resources to strategic business activities such as product expansion and market diversification.

Lessons Learned and Best Practices from Experienced Sellers

1. Lesson Learned 1: Prioritize Customer Experience

Key Takeaway: Providing an exceptional customer experience is paramount in eBay dropshipping. By offering responsive customer support, fast shipping times, and hassle-free returns and refunds, sellers can build trust with buyers, drive repeat business, and establish a positive reputation on the platform.

2. Lesson Learned 2: Diversify Your Product Portfolio

Key Takeaway: Diversifying your product offerings is essential for long-term success in eBay dropshipping. By expanding into complementary product categories, targeting niche markets, and staying ahead of consumer trends, sellers can mitigate risks associated with market fluctuations and capitalize on new revenue opportunities.

3. Lesson Learned 3: Stay Informed About eBay Policies and Updates

Key Takeaway: Staying informed about eBay's policies, updates, and best practices is crucial for maintaining compliance, avoiding account suspensions, and ensuring a smooth selling experience on the platform. Sellers should regularly review eBay's seller policies, participate in seller forums and communities, and stay abreast of industry news and updates to adapt their strategies accordingly.

Conclusion

Congratulations on concluding this comprehensive guide to eBay dropshipping for beginners in 2024. Throughout this journey, we've explored every aspect of starting and running a successful eBay dropshipping business, from understanding the fundamentals to navigating policies and regulations, adapting to changes, and learning from real-life case studies.

Recap of Key Points

Let's take a moment to recap the key points covered in this guide:

1. Understanding eBay Dropshipping: We began by defining eBay dropshipping and exploring why eBay is a popular platform for dropshipping due to its large customer base and seller-friendly policies.

2. Getting Started with eBay Dropshipping:
We discussed the essential steps for getting started, including creating a seller account, researching profitable products, finding reliable suppliers, and understanding eBay's dropshipping policies.

3. Costs of Dropshipping on eBay: We delved into the various costs associated with dropshipping on eBay, including free listings, subscription fees, insertion fees, final value fees, promotional fees, and other budgeting considerations.

4. Setting Up Your eBay Dropshipping Business: We covered topics such as optimizing product listings, managing inventory and orders, fulfilling orders with suppliers, and providing excellent customer service.

5. Strategies for Success: We explored marketing and promotion strategies, building trust and reputation as a seller, pricing strategies for profitability, and tips for efficient operations and growth.

6. *Navigating eBay Policies and Regulations:* We discussed eBay's policies on dropshipping, common mistakes to avoid, and tips for maintaining compliance and avoiding suspension.

7. *Adapting to Changes in 2024:* We examined updates in eBay policies and features, strategies for adapting to market trends and competition, and leveraging new tools and technologies for success.

8. *Case Studies and Success Stories:* We analyzed real-life examples of successful eBay dropshipping businesses and extracted valuable lessons and best practices from experienced sellers.

Final Tips and Recommendations

As you embark on your eBay dropshipping journey, here are some final tips and recommendations to keep in mind:

1. *Continuous Learning:* The world of eCommerce is dynamic and ever-evolving. Stay updated on industry trends, eBay policies, and best practices through continuous learning and participation in seller communities.

2. *Customer-Centric Approach:* Prioritize the needs and satisfaction of your customers. Provide excellent customer service, offer high-quality products, and strive to exceed customer expectations to build a loyal customer base.

3. *Experimentation and Optimization:* Don't be afraid to experiment with different strategies, products, and marketing techniques. Continuously analyze your performance metrics and optimize your approach based on data-driven insights.

4. *Stay Resilient:* Building a successful eBay dropshipping business takes time, effort, and perseverance. Stay resilient in the face of challenges, learn from setbacks, and remain focused on your long-term goals.

5. *Network and Collaborate:* Networking with other sellers, suppliers, and industry professionals can provide valuable opportunities for collaboration, knowledge sharing, and business growth. Attend eCommerce events, join online communities, and seek mentorship from experienced entrepreneurs.

Encouragement for Beginners Embarking on Their eBay Dropshipping Journey

For beginners embarking on their eBay dropshipping journey, remember that every successful entrepreneur started from somewhere. It's okay to start small, make mistakes, and learn along the way. Stay committed to your goals, stay adaptable in the face of changes, and don't hesitate to seek guidance and support when needed.

Believe in yourself, embrace the journey with enthusiasm, and remember that with dedication, hard work, and the right strategies, you have the potential to build a thriving eBay dropshipping business. Best of luck with your entrepreneurial endeavors, and may your eBay dropshipping venture be filled with success and fulfillment.

Appendix

In this appendix, we'll explore essential resources, tools, and information to complement your journey into the world of eBay dropshipping. Whether you're seeking clarification on industry-specific terms, looking for additional tools to streamline your operations, or hoping to find answers to common questions, this section aims to provide valuable insights and resources.

Glossary of Terms

To help you navigate the terminology commonly used in the realm of eBay dropshipping, here's a comprehensive glossary of terms:

1. Dropshipping: A retail fulfillment strategy in which a retailer does not maintain inventory of the goods it sells. Rather, when a shop sells anything, it buys it directly from a third party and ships it straight to the buyer.

2. eBay: An online marketplace where individuals and businesses can buy and sell a wide variety of goods and services worldwide.

3. Supplier: A company or individual that provides products to be sold by a retailer.

4. Seller Account: An account created on eBay that allows individuals and businesses to list items for sale, manage orders, and communicate with buyers.

5. Product Listing: A detailed description of an item for sale, including images, specifications, pricing, and shipping information.

6. Inventory Management: The process of overseeing the ordering, storage, and tracking of a company's inventory.

7. Order Fulfillment: The process of receiving, processing, and delivering orders to customers.

8. Customer Service: The support and assistance provided to customers before, during, and after a purchase.

9. Promotional Fees: Fees paid to eBay for promoting and advertising products on the platform.

10. Final Value Fees: Fees charged by eBay as a percentage of the total sale price of an item.

11. Insertion Fees: Fees charged by eBay for listing items for sale on the platform.

12. Compliance: Adherence to eBay's policies and regulations governing dropshipping activities on the platform.

13. Market Trends: Patterns and shifts in consumer behavior, preferences, and demand within a specific market.

14. Pricing Strategies: Methods used to determine the selling price of products, taking into account factors such as costs, competition, and market demand.

15. Customer Feedback: Reviews and ratings provided by buyers based on their experience with a seller and their products.

16. Suspension: The temporary or permanent restriction of a seller's account on eBay due to policy violations or other infractions.

Additional Resources and Tools

1. eBay Seller Center: An online resource provided by eBay that offers comprehensive guides, tutorials, and tools to help sellers succeed on the platform.

2. *eBay Community Forums:* Online forums where eBay sellers can connect, ask questions, and share experiences with other members of the eBay community.

3. *Dropshipping Suppliers Directory:* Directories and databases of dropshipping suppliers offering a wide range of products across various categories.

4. *Inventory Management Software:* Tools and software solutions designed to streamline inventory management processes, track stock levels, and synchronize inventory across multiple sales channels.

5. *Customer Service Platforms:* Customer service software platforms that enable sellers to manage customer inquiries, messages, and support tickets efficiently.

6. eCommerce Analytics Tools: Analytics tools that provide valuable insights into sales performance, customer behavior, and market trends to inform business decisions.

7. eBay Policy Updates: Stay informed about eBay's latest policy updates, feature releases, and announcements through official eBay communication channels and updates.

Frequently Asked Questions (FAQs)

Q1. Is dropshipping allowed on eBay?
Yes, dropshipping is allowed on eBay as long as sellers adhere to eBay's policies and guidelines regarding dropshipping activities.

Q2. Do I need a business license to dropship on eBay?

While eBay doesn't require sellers to have a business license to sell on the platform, it's essential to comply with any legal requirements in your jurisdiction regarding business registration and taxation.

Q3. How do I find reliable dropshipping suppliers?

Researching and vetting potential suppliers, attending trade shows, networking with industry professionals, and utilizing dropshipping supplier directories are effective ways to find reliable suppliers.

Q4. What are the fees associated with dropshipping on eBay?

Fees may include insertion fees for listing items, final value fees based on the sale price, promotional fees for advertising, and subscription fees for optional seller tools and services.

Q5. How do I handle returns and refunds as a dropshipper on eBay?

As a dropshipper, it's crucial to have clear return and refund policies in place. Coordinate with your suppliers to facilitate returns and refunds efficiently and provide excellent customer service throughout the process.

Q6. How can I optimize my eBay listings for better visibility and sales?

Optimize your listings by using high-quality images, detailed product descriptions, relevant keywords, competitive pricing, and offering fast and reliable shipping options to attract more buyers.

www.ingramcontent.com/pod-product-compliance
Lightning Source LLC
La Vergne TN
LVHW051643050326
832903LV00022B/870